Icon

Icon

Maria Zajkowski

PUNCHER & WATTMANN

First published in 2021

Published by Puncher and Wattmann
PO Box 279
Waratah NSW 2298

http://www.puncherandwattmann.com

puncherandwattmann@bigpond.com

NATIONAL
LIBRARY
OF AUSTRALIA

A catalogue record for this book is available from the National Library of Australia

ISBN   9781922571083

Cover artwork by Liz Rácz

Cover design by Tim Cronin

Printed by Lightning Source International

for my father

To know how much you cannot

It began

And never ended

The sound of the calling to your restless endless zero

Accurately lost

Moving the sun

like moving tears

back into the hawk

Why do you leave the house in the dark

with a thousand black bags

To tie a knot in your lucky escapes

or to put the night to sleep in your heart

I came for the book of wings

in the chapel of lament

the condolence of breath

the prize of missing your life

The solitude of memory

The sceptre of content

Searching for the hierophant

of final journeys

Your moon reveals

a rock's dedication

a spring of stars

In the liquid you write

a temporary letter to last lives

Said and not said

no less said

How to deliver the future to the past

through the needle of an eye

I can't give you dedications

They live their lives on their knees

What means more

than the winter magnetic

Turn all the flowers upside down

One bird watches you on your knees

digging down for the light

Merchants for the symbol

You are dead you say

No, I am carrying this vase

back to the place I was born

Sometimes there are more ways

to be less than the outcome

Are you now listening

to where we were decided?

You lie inside your body

as I lie to mine

The first daffodil of belonging alone

Matchmade to the

loneliness of sense

A moon wanting finally one or the other —

to lose or to die

Our success of absence

Relentless idols burning out of space

asking where you are in this fire

In the divining forest

a future river leaves

a past made empty

We must stop repeating roads

you no longer imagine

to arrive at an end

no destination nears

Beneath the floristry

parts coming apart

Of the thirteen sounds I understood one

a few blank lives before morning

Even the bees that curled in my ears

heard the future disappear between them

And then, the wind

A floating star

in the citadel asks

what comes after

Out from the luminous trees

every breath's forgotten path

What if when

with a flock and an iron bar

you meet two worlds

and have to decide which one will live

Is the distant hammering real

or electric?

All the definitions of *is* do not shift their tiny chains for you

Against the human wind

new angels brace for rapture

The hunger of the futile

Stones on top of stones on top of bread

Then you wish you had

A cup's patience

A knife's peace

All the work of silence

An actual leaf and not the leaf I gave you last night

Secret army

blowing silent horns

no closer to the horizon's

fanfare of flaws

or your voice's diluted absence

My mechanical shortfall

I wear red but am grey

Still covered in insects

looking for the names of the world

In my sleep

I sit at the courage void

listening for a tree to explode

above all things

in a poem

Choir of the strata

where bodies in earth

strike wooden letters

from wooden stars

A last message on the day's branch

Am I lost if you are not looking for loss?

The fool who brings you back

alone with her contribution

Waiting for the statue

to improve the rose

Said to the giant

life is so small

in the empty chimneys

at rest from the living

Dusk

stone exhales

From my night to your night

a plum fortress raises the canyon

Stars come to drink the thin tar of life

To make perfection perfect

the repetition of flaws

Where I point at the horizon

a horizon points back

If nothing is then nothing is

The place where we are joined

does not come here

That would be the river in reverse

You submit to being a repeat

An early cloud noted

as fire under water

What else is there to undecide

when up to your neck in release

Rain percent

Interruptions in the grass

The Icon in the puddle

Did you want

or not want

the overheard results of your heart

The sound of the sky coming

to put you back in your life

Marooned at the fire

of the conditional dream

The natural cause of life is death

Your broken breaths release

the last blue ghosts of day

Wordwind

A queenshaped hope

Scribbling messages to thoughts

do not forget me, I will arrive one night at a time at a time

The kingdom of loneliness

has everything

even a song

So what if no-one hears

From the high tower

loneliness calls

And from below

loneliness answers

So what if no-one knows

they are happy here

The grasses, the barbs

The enormously minute volumes

The waters that ended the cottages of doubt

The desires, the synchronicities

The knocks knocking

The last moments before deaths

The resonant mishearings

The paths across meaning

The crickets adjusting night

who never talked but knew

in my dream there was

a reason for this sleep

How the silent rivers remembered

the soul outside its echo

How the gauze of the window kept

us inside the message

The silver delta met

by the weightless light of life

Between silences

the order of disorder

The layers of eye in your eye

All the beings I cannot be

Small lives forget

and finally find nothing

but the spires of an urgency

too difficult to descend

What explanation moves a frozen howl?

A chair in the room of perfection

Empty

Overloaded

The Walking Past

a bag in its hand

a hat on its head

a bed of lights in the hills

In the other thousand years

we devote our future

to the miles of another altar

Foretold by the chariot wind

at the cracking of the sun

a handful of the tide's empty undecided letters

By the sea of cups

a future escape collects days, thorns, rooves

sheer to the great fading river

everything sees itself in the rain

If the blackbird is singing

I know I am dying

correctly and in tune

It cries the light from its heart

The tide that devours itself

Throwing leaves to the sky

but the sky is gone

Your only wishes

are a different alone

Inside the Icon

the secret

Who is love and who is loved

I cut the grass and plant perfumes

around this perfection

with every other slave to freedom

Still not knowing

the certainties

I reach through the wall

Feel the wind

inside my life

Does this mean I have a meaning?

Or all this specific emptiness

The temple of the clock

The unfinished clouds

Our mutable wreck

The sea's unreachable prayer

Night by night

at the gold fountain

I ask you again

what to forget

You wave so certain

where no thing is nothing

The rapture or the deluge

What comes first

The moon wants to grow

Tired of sitting in our voices

and seeing itself in our eyes

The moon aspires to randomness

unpredictability

fickleness

but never humanity

Just the vanity of something

far less temporary

than a momentary eternity

behind the clouds

Private moebius

the body unmakes the mind

Crossing saints like rivers

suffering relief

The great hall

where you assume liberation

inside the lamplight

of a mouse's eye

I know now sense was just holding our cracks together

The miracle of what doesn't happen here

Stories of birds

we are dumb and call song

while answers all along have been waking us

Do you know you are missing

from your own imitation?

We exchanged the document of the tower

Descending into the words without us

Never meeting what the world said we would

Do you believe in the afterlife

of chances and apologies?

I am sure

in your room

in your body

in your eyes

is the ship I was intending

Thunderscent of the field

Flowers accepting messages

The war between wanting

and wanting to go away

Yellow and purple facts

The necessity of tiny tensions

The sky taking flight

A fire in your head (again)

Final hands arrive

to take you through what cannot be felt

Alone at the arch

You enter light removed

Looking through the windows

of the empty magicians

lights still burning

in the parlours of absence

A glass of arrival

on the future's table

The unreachable experiment of now

Greater than the void

my own giant crown of oblivion

In the blue night

with this wonder of daggers I fall

We came all this way

in another distance to desire

Trapped with what was won

The discomfort of our lives

in the wilderness of the found

Beneath last night's circus

in the background of the quartz

the ghosts around the table wrote

what voice can take our silence

At the altar of the imminent

I stopped below the sword

Is love pairing us adrift?

The statue on the cliff farewells

hearts cut free from sense

as I tune the clocks of night

to the grasses of our final meadow

At the end

I could not find the door

or know the way to our

final moment

You turned inside to say

Is anything woundless?

The sun follows the moon

The child's unteachable discomfort

Your first and last breaths

Eclipsing of the throw by the stone in flight